DISMANTLING ISIS

M. J. ALOHMAYED

For permission to use material from this text or product, suggestion or questions contact M.J.Mohammed1988@gmail.com

For all those who have been oppressed in the name of religion,
who have been murdered, displaced and robbed;

for every woman has been raped;

for every child whose innocence has been replaced with violence and ignorance,

and for everyone defends their rights,

I dedicate this work.

M. J. Alohmayed

I would like to express gratitude and indebtedness to those who assisted and supported me in bringing this book to light. An additional thanks to my friend, whose name will remain untold for the time being, for many useful recommendations and observations, and for being the inspiration for the format of this book.

(Woe, then, unto those who write down, with their own hands, [something which they claim to be] divine writ, and then say. "This is from God," in order to acquire a trifling gain thereby; woe, then, unto them for what their hands have written, and woe unto them for all that they may have gained!) Al-Baqara 79

(Obey me as long as I am among you, then follow the Book Of God, ban what it bans and allow what it allows.) Prophet Muhammad. (Al-Muttaqi,1989: 179)

Introduction to the English edition:

This book was originally written in Arabic, the author's mother tongue. Nevertheless, The need for an English edition was considerable and urgent; especially after many non-Arab Muslims had joined ISIS. Thus, the author, who is also a translator, took the responsibility of rewriting the book in English. This book is not a mere translation of the Arabic edition, but rather a book written for the English readership. Accordingly, there have been differences between the two editions, however, those differences came out of linguistic necessities and cultural specifics; and have been made in a way that kept the primary ideas intact.

Most of the references mentioned in this book are, to the author's best knowledge, only available in Arabic and have not been translated into English yet. Therefore, they have been translated into English by the author. Still, the verses of Quran and Hadith [Prophet Muhammad's sayings] have been quoted from English translations of those books. Concerning Quran, the translation of Mr. Muhammad Asad *The Message of Quran* has been adopted. However, the translation of Quran from Arabic into any other language is a translation of one of the various Quran interpretations. Consequently, the author have made some minor changes to the English verses of Quran quoted in this book so that they accord with his understanding of their original Arabic ones.

Table of Contents

Contents

Preface

A criminal organization known as ISIS has taken over news channels and websites. ISIS is not peculiar to other criminal harmful organizations that were carried away by will to power , but for sure it is the most infamous. History told us about other organizations like ISIS and the horrible things they have done.

However, ISIS is the most dangerous, the wealthiest and the most venomous among its parallels. ISIS stems its power from the ideological currents that justify its actions and give it the potential to continue. Those ideologies have used the religion as a justification to hold sway over people's lives, Negate their rights and wipe out their free will.

Is fighting ISIS militarily enough? Is winning the war against ISIS on the ground only, without fighting its ideology, enough to have an ISIS-free world? The answer to both questions is: No.

We need to track back ISIS ideology to its origins, so as to pull it up by its roots. Then, and only then, we can establish a whole new understanding of the righteous religion rather than mere individuals' interpretations that satisfy clerks desires and fantasies.

This book discusses the actions of ISIS and its fellows, which find their justifications within the books of those clerks. It does not offer a complete Islamic jurisprudence that replaces the current one, rather than discussing the actions of ISIS and other radical organizations. These criminal organizations that got stuck in the body of Islam like a malignant tumor which the observer sees as part and parcel, while the body knows it is nothing of its existence. The book also tackles some of the pretexts that ISIS used to justify devastating the world and perishing the land and people, and then it compares these weak pretexts to Quran. The objective and impartial reader will see the extent of ignorance of those who support these pretexts and, sometimes, their defiance to Quran.

Still, for the prudent truth-seeking readers who are looking for a replacement to this inherited jurisprudence or, at least, a cultivated version of it; I recommend them to review the works of some great thinkers and reformers such as: Gamal Al-Banna, Farag Foda, Nasr Abu Zayd, Ahmed Subhy Mansour, Adnan Ibrahim, Ahmed Maher, Marwan Abdulhadi, Samer Islambouli and Dr. Muhammad Shahrur. These people have spent their lives trying to rectify the inherited Islamic jurisprudence and bring Islam back to the right track

Readers may encounter what would ignite their enthusiasm to defend what they think to be the cornerstone of Islam. To this kind of readers I say: God has given you a brain to use, then He sent His messages –in this case the Quran- in a way your brain can understand and your mind can comprehend:

(And this, too, is a divine writ which We have bestowed from on high, a blessed one: follow it, then, and be conscious of God, so that you might be graced with His mercy (155) It has been given to you] lest you say, "Only unto two groups of people, [both of them] before our time, has a divine writ been bestowed from on high and we were indeed unaware of their teachings" (156) or lest you say, "If a divine writ had been bestowed from on high upon us, we would surely have followed its guidance better than they did." And so, a clear evidence of the truth has now come unto you from your Sustainer, and guidance, and grace. Who, then, could be more wicked than he who gives the lie to God's messages, and turns away from them in disdain? We shall requite those who turn away from Our messages in disdain with evil suffering for having thus turned away!(157)). Al-An'aam 155-157.

So I hereby ask the dear readers to concentrate their enthusiasm to find what is right; and to do that, you need to read with fairness, and above all, you need to skip over the pre-judgment driven by sectarian or doctrinal urges; and, most importantly, to consult your moral constitution.

The book is of three chapters. The first chapter presents a simplified historical account of Hadith (Prophet Muhammad's sayings) writing and collecting, and the criteria that Hadith scholars follow to nominate a Hadith as Sahih (true), and therefore considering it a binding one (the people must do what it says). Then it sheds some light upon the technical problems which undermine the whole Hadith writing thing. Hence, the first chapter will be an introduction to this "discipline" on which ISIS and other criminal organizations build their whole conception and stem their justification to killing everyone will not comply to them, no matter what religion or doctrine they belong to. The second chapter discusses the actions of ISIS in the lands it invaded and violated, using some texts from Quran and Hadith to mislead people and deceive ignorant fervent Muslims elderly and youth. Furthermore, it compares those out-of-context texts to the scientific objective interpretation of Quran to refute their invalid argumentations:

(Verily, they who are bent on denying the truth of this reminder as soon as it comes to them - [they are the losers]: for, behold, it is a sublime divine writ: (41) no falsehood can ever attain to it openly, and neither in a stealthy manner, [since it is] bestowed from on high by One who is truly wise, ever to be praised (42)) Fussilat 41-42

The third chapter shows how ISIS can be dismantled, shedding light on its origin and discuss some steps to obstruct its resurrection. Lastly, it is not enough for a clerk to say that "Sunnah (Mohammed's actions and sayings) does not replace the Quran," whereas his actions show the opposite! Neither it is enough for a Muslim to say that "they do not worship clerks," while they do that in the real life:

(Do they who are bent on denying the truth think, perchance, that they could take [any of] My creatures for protectors against Me? Verily, We have readied hell to welcome all who [thus] deny the truth! (102) Say: "Shall we tell you who are the greatest losers in whatever they may do? (103) "[It is] they whose labour has gone astray in [the pursuit of no more than] this world's life, and who none the less think that they are doing good works: (104)). Al-Kahf 102-104

Chapter 1: The Books of Islamic Heritage

Part 1: The History of Hadith Recording

Writing was not a significant science in Arabian peninsula. Arabic was a spoken rather than a written language; so narrators were roaming the desert between Arabian tribes spreading news and telling tales, and so did poets. Arab's life style before Islam made them in no need to record or write. They did not have a state or empire which would need registers and records that contain, for instance, the names of its soldiers; so the spoken Arabic language was more than enough. In every tribe there was a distinguished figure whose job was to tell them tales and answer their questions about lineages and such things. And so Arabs went on without writing, but rather they depended on reporting one to another and generation to another.

With the beginning of Bi'thah (Muhammad's prophethood) and the beginning of revelation to Muhammad, the recording was a must. The prophet chose several men who knew how to write in Arabic-there were just a few- to copy what has been revealed to him of Quran. Professor Ghanim Qaddouri states in his book *Lectures in Quran Studies*: "The holy Quran has been revealed to the prophet of God while Arabs were mostly illiterate. Alblathiri, while speaking of writing in Makah, said: Islam started when there were only 17 men in Quraish who can write. As for writing in Yathrib (Almadinah) Alblathiri said: Islam started while there were several men who can write, and he counted 11 men. Ibn Qutaiba said: there were few Arabs who can write." (2003: 49).

Recording kept limited to a certain class and for a certain kind of things such as trading contracts and state registers which has been included during the time of Omar Ibn Al-khattab[1]. "The materials that early Arabs used for writing included: reed pen and lampblack ink. Arabs were writing on palm branches after they scraped their frond, camel bones, potsherds, small white stones, leather, parchment and Egyptian papyrus as sheet of papers. The use of Egyptian papyrus is the first for Arabs, and that was after conquering Egypt 20 years following Hijra (when Muhammad moved from Makkah to Almadinah", according to Jumaa Ibrahim in his *The Story of Arabic Writing* (1989: 39-40).

Arabs used to share knowledge, including The Sunnah, via spoken language. Even those who wrote down the Prophet's sayings and commandments, they did that only until they memorized them. After memorizing, they would erase and shred what they had written in obedience to the Prophet and the caliphs commands (as shown in part 3 of this chapter) to not write but the Quran in order for people not to take these sayings as a reference or

---

[1] Omar Ibn Al-Khattab (577-644) was the second (Caliph) successor of Prophet Muhammad. He ruled the Islamic State from 634 to 644.

source of Islamic Jurisprudence, which has unfortunately been happening for the last 1400 years.

However, without going further into somewhat-known historical information, let's read some historical facts that have been missed, or concealed, and have not had the circulation they deserve. Those are the time gaps in recording Sunnah; as what Georges Awad, a member of Iraqi scientific community, reveals in his *Oldest Arabic Scripts in the Libraries of the World, which are written from early Islam to year 500 H :*

The scripts with the numbers 303, 304, 305 , are under the title "Al-Jamii Al-Sahih", also known as "Sahih Al-Bukhari"[2]. The oldest of the three scripts is dated back to the year 407

---

[2] It is one of the six major Hadith collections in Sunni Islam, and the most authentic Hadith collection. It is highly acclaimed by Sunni Muslims as well as Zaidi Shia Muslims. Some Sunni Muslims consider Sahih Al-Bukhari as the most authentic book after Quran.

H without a reference to its writer; whereas Al-Bukhari[3] died in 256 H.

The script number 476 under the title "Sahih Muslim"[4], is dated 368 H, whereas Imam Muslim[5] died in 261 H.

Scripts number 417, 418, 419, under the title "Al-Sunan" by Al-Nisa'i[6]; the oldest of them dated to 355 H, whereas Al-nisa'i died in 303 H.

The script number 421, under the title "Al-Sunan" by Al-Darqatni[7] is dated back to the

---

[3] Muhammad Ibn Ismael Al-Bukhari (810-870) was a Persian Islamic scholar who authored the Hadith collection.

[4] It is one of the six major Hadith collections in Sunni Islam, and the second most authentic Hadith collection after Sahih Al-Bukhari. It is highly acclaimed by Sunni Muslims as well as Zaidi Shia Muslims.

[5] Muslim Ibn Al-Ḥajjāj (815-875) was a Persian Islamic scholar who authored the Hadith collection.

[6] Ahmed Ibn Shu'ayb Al-Nisa'I (829-915) was an Islamic scholar who authored the Hadith collection. His book "Al-Sunan" is considered by Sunni Muslims as one of the major six Hadith Collections.

fifth century of Hijra; whereas AL-Darqatni died in 385 H. (1982: 112-113, 147-148, 165)

So the questions are: Who wrote Sahih Al-Bukhari? Who wrote Sahih Muslim? Who wrote the books of Sunnah? Why is there such a chronological gap between their death and the recording of their books? And why we can find the scripts of Quran written by Othman bin Affan[8] and Ali Bin Abi Talib[9], even though they were written centuries prior to the period in which Hadith has been recorded? Why have not Al-Bukhari himself wrote what he has collected? Is it really possible for Muslims to depend on writers about whom they know nothing; and, consequently, build a

---

[7] Ali Ibn Omar Al-Darqatni (919-995) was an Islamic scholar who authored the Hadith collection. His book "Al-Sunan" is considered by Sunni Muslims as one of the major six Hadith Collections.

[8] Othman Ibn Affan (577-656) was the third (Caliph) successor of Prophet Muhammad. He ruled the Islamic State from 644 to 656.

[9] Ali Ibn Abi Talib (600?-661) was the fourth (Caliph) successor of Prophet Muhammad. Heruled the Islamic State from 656-661. He is believed to be the first male Muslim child.

whole religion on nothing but a guess? Since God has not promised to reserve Hadith, as He did with Quran: **(Behold, it is We Ourselves who have bestowed from on high, step by step, this reminder(The Qur'an) and, behold, it is We who shall truly guard it [from all corruption]. (9))** Al-Hijr. No clerk or scholar should argue that what we have now of Prophet Muhammad's sayings are sacred, or that these sayings were not liable for cheating, careless omission and unintentional mistakes.

Part 2: Hadith Sahih (True sayings):

In this part of the chapter we will discuss some terms of Hadith, on which most Islamic Jurisprudence has been based. What is a true prophet's saying? Is it the one that agrees with Quran? And whether it is eligible to derive commandments from or not.

Mahmud AL-Tahhan, a professor in Hadith, says in his book *Simplifying the Term of Hadith*, describing the true sayings: "3- Terms of Eligibility: we can see from the definition that the five terms of eligibility are: a connected chain of transmission, uprightness of narrators, verification of narrators, absence of blemish and absence of eccentricity. In case of the absence of one of these terms, a saying is not true." According to this, a saying's opposition to Quran is not a term of its eligibility! In his definition of eccentricity Al-Tahhan says: "Eccentricity is when a saying narrated by a verified narrator is opposing another saying narrated by more verified narrator." So, a saying is challenged as false when it opposes another saying, but not when opposing Quran! (1995:31).

AL-Tahhan further describes the authority of a true saying: "5- Its authority: it is obligatory to obey what is in it, as Hadith scholars and reliable clerks and jurisprudence experts have unanimously agreed, for it is (true saying) a pretext of legislation, and a Muslim cannot deny it." (Ibid: 32).

From this perspective, no Muslim can deny a Hadith such as this one:
"Anas Ibn Malik[10] reported that a person asked God's Apostle:

When would the Last Hour come? Thereupon God's Messenger (May peace be upon him) kept quiet for a while. Then he looked at a young boy in his presence belonging to the tribe of AzdShanu'a and said: If this boy lives he would not grow very old till the Last Hour

---

[10] Anas Ibn Malik (612-709 or 712) was a companion of Prophet Muhammad. According to Sunni Muslims, Anas is one of the major and most authentic narrators of Hadith

would come. Anas said that this young boy was of our age during those days." (Sahih Muslim, 2006: 1351).

Apart from all the fabrication and decoration being laid by heritage worshipers, this "true saying" presents two problems: 1- the hour of doom has not come till now. We cannot accept this saying unless the boy mentioned in it is still alive without getting very old. 2- this saying, and others like it, are clearly opposing Quran. If we agreed, hypothetically, that their manipulative justifications do not deny the bless of reason; should not the prophet obey the orders of God and say: I do not acquire such knowledge. God only knows when it is:

(THEY WILL ASK thee [O Prophet] about the Last Hour: "When will it come to pass?" Say: "Verily, knowledge thereof rests with my Sustainer alone. None but He will reveal it in its time. Heavily will it weigh on the heavens and the earth; [and] it will not fall upon you otherwise than of a sudden." They will ask thee - as if thou

couldst gain insight into this [mystery] by dint of persistent inquiry! Say:"Knowledge thereof rests with my Sustainer alone; but [of this] most people are unaware. (187)). Al-A'araaf 187

This verse, among others, shows that the time of the last hour is something hidden and God has not revealed it to his prophet; whereas a traditional understanding is on the contrary of this.

Another example that shows how "true" prophet's sayings are opposing Quran is this saying in the books of Al-Bukhari and Muslim:

"Narrated by Anas:

That the Meccan people requested God's Messenger to show them a miracle, and so he showed them the splitting of the moon so they can see the mount of Hiraa" (Sahih Al-Bukhāri,1998:659); (Sahih Muslim, 2006: 1290).

Despite, God has said: **(and so they say: "[O Muhammad,] we shall not believe thee till thou cause a spring to gush forth for us from the earth,(90) or thou have a garden of date-palms and vines and cause rivers to gush forth in their midst in a sudden rush,(91) or thou cause the skies to fall down upon us in smithereens, as thou hast threatened, or [till] thou bring God and the angels face to face before us,(92) or thou have a house [made] of gold, or thou ascend to heaven - but nay, we would not [even] believe in thy ascension unless thou bring down to us [from heaven] a writing which we [ourselves] could read! Say thou, [O Prophet:] "Limitless in His glory is my Sustainer! Am I, then, aught but a mortal man, an apostle?" (93)).** Al-Israa' 90-93

In this verse God clearly tells Prophet Muhammad to answer those who ask him to show them miracles by telling them that he is not but a mortal man, an apostle of God, and that he has no miracles nor he has super powers but a message from his Creator to deliver.

Part 3: Did Prophet Muhammad and his Successors Allow Recording Hadith?

Prophet Muhammad forbid recording Hadith. There are several sayings, if they have truly been said by the prophet, that directly forbid writing and recording Hadith, such as:

1- *Abu Sa'eed Khudri[11] reported that God's Messenger said:*

"Do not take down anything from me, and he who took down anything from me except the Qur'an should efface that and narrate from me, for there is no harm in it. And he who

---

[11] Abu Sa'eed Khudri (?-684 or 693) was a companion of Prophet Muhammad. According to Sunni Muslims, Abu Sa'eed is one of the major and most authentic narrators of Hadith.

attributed any falsehood to me-and Hammam said: I think he also said:" deliberately" -he should in fact find his abode in the Hell-Fire ".(Sahih Muslim,2006:1366).

2- Narrated by Abu Sa'eed Al-Khudri:

"We sought permission from the Messenger of God for writing but he did not permit us". (Al-Tirmithi,1999: 431).

3- Al-Muttalib Ibn Abdullah Ibn Hantab said: Zayd Ibn Thabit[12] entered upon Mu'awiyah[13] and asked him about a tradition. He ordered a man to write it. Zayd said: The Messenger of God ordered us not to write any of his traditions. So he erased it. (Al-Sajistāni,1999: 403)

4-Abu Bakr[14] summoned the people right after Prophet Muhammad's death, addressing

---

[12] Zayd Ibn Thabit (?-665) was a companion of Prophet Muhammad.
[13] Muʿāwiyah ibn ʾAbī Sufyān (602-680) was a companion of Prophet Muhammad and his brother-in-law. He established the Umayyad Dynasty of the caliphate,[1][2] and was the second caliph from the Umayyad clan, the first being Othman Ibn Affan.

them: "you speak to people [about God's messenger tradition] of things you contradict each other with them, and the people after you will contradict even more. Transfer nothing of God's Messenger sayings, and if you are asked, answer by saying: we have the Book of God [Quran]; ban what it has banned and allow what it has allowed." (Al-Thahabi,1374: 2-3).

5- "Abu Salama reported when asking Abu Huraira[15]: have you been narrating about God's messenger during Omar's reign as you are doing now? Abu Huraira answered: if I was narrating during Omar's reign as I am doing now, he would have hit me with his cane." (Ibid: 12).

---

[14] Abdullah Ibn Abi Qhuhafah (known as Abu Bakr) (573-634) was the first (Caliph) successor of Prophet Muhammad. He ruled the Islamic State from 632-634. He is believed to be the first male Muslim adult.
[15] Abd ar-Raḥmān Ibn Ṣakhr Ad-Dawsī Al-Azdī (Known as Abu Huraira) (603-681) was a companion of Prophet Muhammad. According to Sunni Muslims, Abu Huraira is the most authentic and prolific narrator of Hadith.

6- "Shuba reported on the authority of Asaad Bin Ibrahim on the authority of his father that Omar locked three men, Ibn Masoud, Abu Addrdaa' and Abu Masoud Al-Ansari and said to them: You had narrated too much about God's messenger." (Ibid: 12).

Additionally, There are many sayings of the prophet and his followers that strongly recommend not to write down his tradition and include it as a part of the religion. He ordered to burn or erase and get rid of what they have written. His caliphs did so as well; for they knew what dissentious books, apart from Quran, would be. Their fears were realized; people deserted the Quran to what has nothing to do with Muhammad's version of religion. They invented a religion which is based on hatred and aggression, then they call it "Sunnah" or Prophet Muhammad's tradition; God forbid this is the prophet's tradition! However, there will be lots of objections by those who have not read Quran and those who have read Quran with the eye of clerks and received it through their minds. Such people will object in fury and say "Without the books of Sunnah we would have not known how to perform prayers." To those we say:

1- Revisit the books of Sunnah and you will be surprised by the amount of contradiction they carry.

2- Performing prayers and giving Zakat (a tax given by Muslims and distributed over poor and the ones in need) are continuously recurrent, i.e., Muslims have not stopped performing prayers since the time of Prophet Muhammad until this day. One generation after the other has performed prayers with almost perfect unanimity among Muslims; whereas the prophet's sayings have only several narrators to tell them, and in some cases only one narrator.

3- Dr. Muhammad Shahrour, an Islamic reformer, states in his article *A Comment on the Books, Articles and Responses to "The Book & The Quran: Contemporary Reading,"* that: "God has created the universe and formed the revelation; and we must see the unity of the Creator in both of them. The unity which is revealed in giving everything a certain role. In fact, there is nothing irrelevant in the universe, and so God formed the revelation, without redundancy. We cannot omit a word and still get the same meaning, nor a word can precede another without affecting the intended meaning (not merely the aesthetic value of the text or its musical harmony). Let's read: **(And perform prayers and give zakat and obey the Messenger - that you may receive mercy.)** 56 al-Noor. If we put the verse in the following word order: (and obey the Messenger and perform prayers and give Zakat- that you may receive mercy.), we would get a whole new meaning, even though the three orders are still there: preform prayers, give Zakat and Obey the Messenger.

We understand from the verse in its new word order, after fronting and backgrounding, that God is ordering us to always Obey the messenger and in everything, and that He is ordering us to perform a prayer that we already know how to perform and give Zakat that we already know how to give. If we apply this understanding to the revelation, the verse would be a wrong statement, God forbid, since there is no hint in the whole revelation on how to perform prayers with its standing, sitting, kneeling and prostration, nor there is explanation on what amounts of money one should pay for Zakat and when to give it. Hence, we understand that God is ordering us to obey the messenger in performing prayers and giving Zakat, which God knows that He does not explain them comprehensively in the revelation".

*It is worth noting that the verse mentioned above is the only verse in which the order is to obey the messenger solely, without God, and it is only in performing prayers and giving Zakat.

Moreover, others may take verses that are extracted out of their context as an argument to put the obedience to the prophet before obedience to God, such as: **(Hence, accept [willingly] whatever the Apostle gives you [thereof], and refrain from [demanding] anything that he withholds from you; and remain conscious of God: for, verily, God is severe in retribution).** Indeed, the verse in its full context is as follows: **(Whatever [spoils taken] from the people of those villages God has turned over to His Apostle - [all of it] belongs to God and the Apostle, and the near of kin [of deceased believers], and the orphans, and the needy, and the wayfarer, so that it may not be [a benefit] going round and round among such of you as may [already] be rich. Hence, accept [willingly] whatever the Apostle gives you [thereof], and refrain from [demanding] anything that he withholds from you; and remain conscious of God: for, verily, God is severe in retribution.(7)).** Al-Hashr

Reading these examples thoroughly, one can see how the lack of understanding Quran and the inability to see what lies beyond the words drove early scholars, clerks and even ordinary people to report sayings and attribute them to the Prophet. Their misplaced enthusiasm pushed them to echo antecedent nations' mythologies and Ordinances that contradict what is in Quran. Muhammad's tradition really was following Quran's teachings and guidelines!

Chapter 2: ISIS' Actions

Part 1: The Islamic State

The Islamic State or The State of Islam are the titles under which ISIS and the like are committing their evil deeds and legalizing their crimes. Oddly, there are no such titles through the history of political Islam; we have heard of an Omayyad Empire, an Abbasside Empire, an Ottoman Empire, the Ayyubid State, and other states which made use of religion to expand their territories and control peoples' minds and lives. These states held the names of the ruling dynasties but never Islam. Such states employed every means possible to expand, control and rule; except Shura (CONSULITATING people concerning the state's affair) contradicting the teachings of Quran. And since Islamic-state-is-a-must adherents have no legitimate argument defending their claims (From Quran or heritage books), they resorted to de facto policies and forbade even questioning the matter.

ISIS Arguments Supporting their Claims to an Islamic State (From Quran):

1- **(Judge, then, between the followers of earlier revelation in accordance with what God has bestowed from on high, and do not follow their errant views, forsaking the truth that has come unto thee)** Al-Maa'edah 48. They, ISIS jurists, present this part of the verse as follows: **(Rule, then, the followers of earlier revelation in accordance with what God has bestowed from on high, and do not follow their errant views, forsaking the truth that has come unto thee).** Unsurprisingly, they do not complete the verse in which it is mentioned that **(Unto every one of you have We appointed a [different] law and way of life. And if God had so willed, He could surely have made you all one single community).** There is no

reference to an Islamic state or caliphate as
ISIS but its theorists want people to believe,
neither in this verse nor in any other part of
the Quran.

2- **(O you who have attained to faith! Pay
heed unto God, and pay heed unto the
Apostle and unto those from among
you who have been entrusted with
authority)** Al-Nisaa' 59. They claim, falsely,
that this verse is a reference to a Muslim ruler
of an Islamic state; whereas it refers, again, to
judging between people; and here is the
context: **(BEHOLD, God bids you to deliver
all that you have been entrusted with unto
those who are entitled thereto, and
whenever you judge between people, to
judge with justice. Verily, most excellent is
what God exhorts you to do: verily, God is
all-hearing, all-seeing! (58) O you who have
attained to faith! Pay heed unto God, and
pay heed unto the Apostle and unto those
from among you who have been entrusted
with authority; and if you are at variance**

over any matter, refer it unto God and the Apostle, if you [truly] believe in God and the Last Day. This is the best [for you], and best in the end.(59). Those "from among you who have been entrusted with authority" is a very clear reference to the people whom we gave them our trust, the people we chose to put them in charge; a manager in his office, a commander in his base and a government we voted for. In these terms, we have the judicial system to settle our disagreement, since the ultimate goal of litigation is for people to get their rights. The judicial system guarantees the rights of people, and it is more likely, nowadays, for a person to get his rights in a non-Islamic state than in the so-called Islamic states.

ISIS Arguments Supporting their Claims to an Islamic State (Books of Islamic Heritage):

1- Ibn Omar[16] said: Prophet Muhammad said:

"The one who withdraws his band from obedience (to the Ruler) will find no argument (in his defense) when he stands before God on the Day of Judgment, and the one who dies without having bound himself by an oath of allegiance (to the ruler) will die the death of one belonging to the days of Jahillyya (the state of ignorance of God's guidance)" (Sahih Muslim,2006:898).

This saying, if it was truly said by the prophet, does not make any reference at all to an Islamic state. However, it asserts on giving the oath of allegiance; which simply means to

---

[16] Abdullah Ibn Omar Ibn Al-Khattab (614-693) was a companion of Prophet Muhammad. According to Sunni Muslims, Ibn Omar is one of the most authentic narrators of Hadith. and he was one of the earliest Muslim scholars.

vote and have a word in **deciding** who is going to rule. There are other sayings that are falsely attributed to Prophet Muhammad which are fabricated and promoted during the rule of Omayyad and Abbasside empires. Such sayings call for blind obedience to the ruler even if he was an unjust tyrant as long as he is a Muslim tyrant! A heritage like that made of Muslims subservient enslaved people.

2- Drawing an analogy between the Islamic state and the unanimity of prophet Muhammad's followers to choose a successor after his death. It may be a social, political and religious duty for people to choose a leader whether it is a person or a council; **since doing so guarantees the** wellbeing of the countries and people. However, there is no obligation whatsoever for people to establish a state in the name of Islam. Islam is a religion, and a religion is a **set of beliefs that** one holds in his mind and not in a state with borders.

Establishing Islamic State has been the wining card for power-hungry people for so long. They have been trying to make it a fundamental part of religion. Here is a part of an article by Taha Hussein[17] written in 1925 following the expel of Ali Abdulraziq from Al-Azhar Islamic University after the publish of the latter's book (Islam and the Fundamentals to Rule):

"And what have you said in this book? You have said that Caliphate is not fundamental to Islam; would you complete the research and finalize the theory? Caliphate is not fundamental to Islam, however, it is fundamental to Roman jurisprudence... you will see that Caliphate for Muslims is nothing but the positions of the Roman Empire, and the Caliph is a mere emperor and the governmental positions of the Islamic state are not but the governmental positions of the Roman Empire." Cited in (Hasan,2012:44)

---

[17] Taha Hussein (1889-1973) was an Egyptian literary figure, thinker, and critic; one of the pioneers of modernism in Arabic Literature.

Part 2: Invasion

There is more than one justification in ISIS' logic for invading other people's lands and taking control over their lives; the most common one is that their victims to be "unbelievers". The term "unbeliever" is not specifically used to describe a non-Muslim: as long as you do not believe in the ISIS version of Islam you are an unbeliever. Being an unbeliever gives ISIS, according to them, the divine right to take your land, enslave you and your family and murder you if you show any resistance. Invasion was never a holy war in Islam, but it was holy in political Islam and the Islamic states and empires; after all, what is better than religion to drive people to war?!

ISIS Arguments for the Legitimacy of Invasion (from Quran):

1- **(And so, when the sacred months are over , kill those who ascribe divinity to aught beside God wherever you may come upon them, and take them captive, and besiege them, and lie in wait for them at every conceivable place ! Yet if they repent, and take to prayer, and render the purifying dues, let them go their way: for, behold, God is much forgiving, a dispenser of grace.)** Al-Tawba 5.

This verse is, as other verses, extracted out of its context to give the murderers a justification for slaying people. The context of the verse is referring to the heads of the unbelievers between whom and Prophet Muhammad there was a covenant not to attack one another which they broke it. The preceding verse tells the prophet and his followers to fulfill their obligation to the ones who have not betrayed them: **(But excepted** shall be -from among those who ascribe divinity to aught beside God - [people] with whom you [O believers] have made a covenant and who thereafter have in no wise failed to fulfill their obligations towards you, and neither have aided anyone against you: observe, then, your covenant with them until the end of the term agreed with them. Verily, God loves those who are conscious of Him.) AL-Tawba 4.

2- Another out of context verse they use to justify their criminal actions is:(**And kill them wherever you may come upon them, and drive them away from wherever they drove you away - for oppression is even worse than killing. And fight not against them near the Inviolable House of Worship unless they fight against you there first; but if they fight against you, kill them: such shall be the recompense of those who deny the truth.**) Al-Baqara 191.

Again, they take advantage of the illiterates and the ignorant by trying to hide what does not go in concord with their purposes such as the verse preceding the one above, which is: **(And fight in God's cause against those who wage war against you, but do not commit aggression-for, verily, God does not love aggressors.)** Al-Baqara 190. It is so obvious how the so-called Islamic states have been able to enlist millions and millions of men to wage wars against peaceful people by simply hiding the truth. The verse clearly tells Muslims not to start a war; but that did not suit the rulers nor their courts and the generously paid clerks so they manipulated the people employing brainwash tactics.

ISIS Arguments for the Legitimacy of Invasion (Books of Islamic Heritage):

1- Narrated by Ibn 'Umar:

God's Messenger said: *"I have been ordered (by God) to fight against the people until they testify that none has the right to be worshipped but God and that Muhammad is God's Messenger, and offer the prayers perfectly and give the obligatory charity (Zakat).So if they perform that, they will save their lives and property from me except for Islamic laws. After that, their reckoning (accounts) will be done by God."* (Sahih Al-Bukhāri,1998: 28).

This saying has in no way been said by the prophet since it contradicts what is asserted by Quran:

(And [thus it is:] had thy Sustainer so willed, all those who live on earth would surely have attained to faith, all of them: dost thou, then,[O Prophet] think that thou couldst compel people to believe) Younus 99. And thus we ask ISIS and all the fundamentalist scholars and clerks: do you think you could compel people to believe?! The Quran also says: **(And so, [O Prophet,] exhort them; thy task is only to exhort: (21)thou canst not compel them [to believe]).** Al-Ghashyia 21-22. The essential base of Islam is freedom; a concept not included in the dictionary of ISIS and its likes: **(There shall be no coercion in matters**

of faith. Distinct has now become the right way from [the way of] error..) Al-Baqara 256. So it is clear that neither ISIS nor any other faith trader could, then, impose their version of what is right or good or decide who is going to heaven or hell. Freedom is the backbone of Islam, and it is guaranteed for all humans. Whether you are a Muslim, Christian, Jew, agnostic or an atheist; one is free to believe in what they want. Other people have no religious obligation to impose their beliefs on you; in fact, they have an obligation NOT to. This argument is the same against the punishment of Apostasy (as we will discuss in part 6 of this chapter).

Part 3: Slavery

"Before Shaytān [The devil] reveals his doubts to the weak-minded and weak hearted, one should remember that enslaving the families of the kuffār [Unbelievers] and taking their women as concubines is a firmly established aspect of the Sharī'ah [Jurisprudence] that if one were to deny or mock, he would be denying or mocking the verses of the Qur'ān and the narrations of the Prophet (sallallāhu 'alayhi wa sallam), and thereby apostatizing from Islam". This is from an article published by DABIQ, ISIS' official magazine, defending ISIS kidnapping Yazidi women and children after invading Sinjar (a hometown of Yazidi minority northern Iraq) and killing or displacing thousands of innocent people (2014: 14).

Enslaving people is not of a much difference from the subject of Caliphate or The Islamic State; they both share the same amount of wrongdoing by people and freedoms denying. However, motifs to each are different. Whereas the concept of the Islamic State was put to feed the hunger to power, Slavery is to fulfill the sexual desires of the twisted minds who legitimated it, and also to drive more men to fight in the name of the ruler. The two concepts, Slavery and the Islamic state, also share the feature of being without any evidence from the Quran.

ISIS Arguments for Slavery (from Quran):

The ill interpretation of this Verse **(other than those whom you rightfully possess)** Al-Nisaa 24. Islamic scholars claim that this verse is about female captives, the married once precisely, and how they are no longer considered married after being enslaved during war, thus their captivators will be free to have them as concubines.

There is no evidence in Quran that legislates enslaving women and children whatever was the cause of war. In fact, Quran restricts those who have not been killed by Muslims during war to one single status, prisoners of war. Two things to keep in mind about a lawful war captivity: 1- Muslim cannot captivate peaceful innocent people who have not fought Muslims. 2- Captivating people, including warriors, is not permitted if the war was not a defensive one.

As for the controversial term "Rightfully Possessed," it is what some Islamic scholars used to sexually abuse and rape women, satisfying their twisted desires. ISIS revived the "sex slavery" by forcing enslaved women to be concubines. The term "Rightfully Possessed" is mentioned in Quran, referring to both males and females, always associated with consent: **(And to those who seek marriage with those whom you rightfully possess: marry them [with their consent] if you are aware of any good in them: and give them their share of the wealth of God** which He has given you. And do not, in order to gain some of the fleeting pleasures of this worldly life, coerce your maidens into whoredom if they happen to be desirous of marriage; and if anyone should coerce them, then, verily, after they have been compelled [to submit in their helplessness], God will be much-forgiving, a dispenser of grace!) Al-Noor 33.

ISIS Arguments for Slavery (Books of Islamic Heritage):

The Juristic reasoning by analogy on the Invasion of Banu Qurayza[18] according to the books of Islamic heritage. Banu Qurayza violated their agreement with Muslims after the latter were attacked by their enemy (Quraish[19] and Ghatfan[20]), and Banu Qurayza

---

[18] A Jewish tribe that was living in Madinah with Muslims

[19] Quraish was a powerful merchant Arabian tribe that controlled Mecca.

[20] Banu Ghatfan was a massive ancient tribe north of Madinah.

agreed to give Quraish and Ghatfan a safe passage into Madinah through their stronghold. Anyway, the story as told by the books of Islamic Heritage states that after winning the battle Muslims held a siege on Banu Qurayza's stronghold. Banu Qurayza agreed that they would surrender to Saad Bin Muath[21] (their former ally). Saad Bin Muath, according to heritage books, gave sentence that men are to be killed and women and children to be enslaved. Additionally, there is the saying that is attributed to prophet Muhammad to give legitimacy to slavery: *"You ruled by God's rule form above seven heavens."* (Al-Ghazāli, 2000: 242).

This story contradicts what is stated in Quran about the incident: **(Thus, for all their fury, God repulsed those who were bent on denying the truth; no advantage did they gain, since God was enough to [protect] the believers in battle - seeing that God is most**

---

[21] Saad Ibn Muath (590?-627) was the chief of the Banu Aus tribe in Madina and one of the prominent companions of Prophet Muhammad.

**powerful, almighty;(25) and He brought
down from their strongholds those of the
followers of earlier revelation[Banu
Qurayza] who had aided the
aggressors, and cast terror into their
hearts: some you killed, and some you
made captive;(26))** Al-Ahzaab 25-26.

To sum up, there is no mention of what
may legitimize enslaving people in Quran.
However, enslaving people, women and
children in particular, is a past nations'
tradition, which Arab empires (Omayyad,
Abbasside...) have attached to religion
putting a divine aspect to it. The term
"Rightfully possessed," refers in no way to
what conceived to be a permission by Quran
promoting taking women as concubines. A
contextual reading through the verses in
which the term "Rightfully Possessed" has
been mentioned would show how far some
Islamic scholars have gone in shaping Islam
to look somewhat like their ethnical and

regional traditions.

Part 4: Murdering Captives

Sweeping the news channels, we all have seen headlines such as "ISIS Murdered a Reporter who has been Taken Captive…" What many people do not know is that being a non-Muslim reporter did not complicate those poor victims situation. It does not matter whether you are Muslim, Arab or civilian; as long as you disagree with ISIS, your "rightful" punishment would be death!

People who have been taken into captivity by ISIS are not war prisoners. Rather, they are hostages who have been kidnapped by a criminal organization and therefore, the international community is obliged to fight for freeing them and bring their kidnappers to justice.

ISIS' Arguments for Murdering Captives (From Quran):

There is no single verse, including out of context ones, in the whole Quran that gives any sort of permission for murdering captives. However, there is a story-which ,judging by its contradictions, one can safely assume to be bogus- about a verse of Quran: **(It does not behoove a prophet to keep captives unless he has battled strenuously on earth. You [O believers] may desire the fleeting gains of this world-but God desires [for you the good of] the life to come: and God is almighty, wise.)** Al-Anfaal 67. And here is the story as told by books of Islamic heritage: Following the battle of Badr, Muslims took captives from Quraish. Prophet Muhammad asked his followers for their opinions concerning those captives. Abu Bakr suggested that they either bestow captives their freedom, or they can take a ransom in return for letting them go. Omar Ibn Al-Khattab, on the other hand, suggested that they should kill the captives. Prophet

Muhammad chose to give the captives their freedom back, which was not what God wanted so He revealed this verse admonishing the prophet's decision of not killing the captives. This story is, poorly, made up; and for two reasons:

1- The claim that God admonished prophet Muhammad not killing the captives contradicts what is told by the same heritage books. This is so because an argument for murdering captives(Discussed in the next paragraph) that prophet Muhammad killed some of the captives of the battle of Badr has been made.

2- The context of the verse is in no way admonishing keeping the captives alive: **(It does not behoove a prophet to keep captives unless he has battled strenuously on earth. You may desire the fleeting gains of this world-but God desires [for you the good of] the life to come: and God is almighty, wise... O Prophet, say unto the**

captives who are in your hands: "If
God finds any good in your hearts,
He will give you something better
than all that has been taken from
you, and will forgive you your sins:
for God is much-forgiving, a
dispenser of grace.") Al-Anfaal 67,70.

ISIS' Argument for Murdering Captives (Books of Islamic Heritage):

Mar'i A. Mar'i, Assistant Professor in
Islamic studies, states in his *Ordinances of
Mujahedeen in the Cause of God in Islamic
Jurisprudence* that:"Scholars have agreed
unanimously, as far as I know, on that the
ruler of Muslims has the right to kill enemy
captives as he sees necessary; for God has
said in Quran:
'kill those who ascribe divinity to aught
beside God,' and he also said 'Thus, if anyone
commits aggression against you, attack him

just as he has attacked you.' And Prophet Muhammad has killed some captives of the battle of Badr." (Mar'i, 2003: 438).

Nonetheless, Mr. Mar'i did not state what is the benefit in murdering captives who have no power so they may be considered as threat to the state in question. The verses Mr. Mar'i quoted have been discussed in the previous parts of this chapter; and have no reference whatsoever to the topic of captives and the crime of murdering them. Furthermore, the claims, such as Mr. Mar'i's, that Prophet Muhammad has killed captives contradict the claim that God admonished prophet Muhammad for not killing captives.

Finally, captives in Islam have two ordinances and nothing more, as Quran ordered; The first: Bestowing them their freedom. The second: giving them their freedom in return for something; money or captives. These two ordinances are valid during the war only, i.e., if the war is over, captives should be released unconditionally, unless there is a special case, for example there are Muslim captives whom the enemy has not let go yet.

Part 5: Jizyah

Jizyah is an exemption poll tax levied by Islamic states on their non-Muslim subjects throughout history. Islamic jurisprudence made it clear that a non-Muslim citizen, especially a Christian or a Jew, living in a territory that lies under an Islamic state's influence has to pay the Jizyah in order to practice their religion freely, as well as for protection from an outer aggression.

In fact, It is unclear when Jizyah was first levied, but the best guess is that it started after Islamic state expanded during the rule of prophet Muhammad's successors. There was not a definition for our modern day taxing system; and Quran only mentioned Zakat (which is the taxation of income and wealth of a Muslim. It is a form of obligatory alms giving, and the collected amount is paid to poor, to zakat collectors, to new converts to Islam, to freeing slaves and captives, to those who are indebted, to military preparations against an aggressor and to those who are away from home.) Zakat is a tax imposed only on Muslims; and after the expansion of the Islamic States there were non-Muslims living under the Muslim's rule, a problem for the Islamic jurisprudence that must be solved. The best solution scholars could come up with was Jizyah. Jizyah was a kind of taxation system for people of religions other than Islam who lived in Islamic state.

However, Jizyah was never a commandment of Islam that, as ISIS suggests, if one questions its validity, they are rejecting the bases of Islam. imposing Jizyah now, as ISIS did with the Christian of Iraq, is nothing but abusing the texts to get money enabling them to expand their criminal activities.

ISIS' Argument for Imposing Jizyah (from Quran):

([And] fight against those who - despite having been vouchsafed revelation [aforetime] -do not [truly] believe either in God or the Last Day, and do not consider forbidden that which God and His Apostle have forbidden, and do not follow the religion of truth [which God has enjoined upon them] till they [agree to] pay Jizyah [the exemption tax] with a willing hand, after having been humbled [in war].) Al-Tawba29.

The verse above is the only position in Quran where Jizyah is mentioned. Scholars and ISIS theorists would present this verse without referring to the most fundamental condition of Jizyah; which is: the exemption tax is only levied on an aggressor warring force.

Furthermore, The context of revelation of this verse is the Battle of Tabouk against the Byzantine Empire. Here is the story according to *Ar-Rahīq al-Makhtum* (2007:429,430,431,435), a modern Islamic Hagiography of Prophet Muhammad written by the Indian Muslim author Safiur Rahman Mubarakpuri,: The reason for the war against the Byzantine Empire was the death of one ofProphet Muhammad's ambassadors at the hands of Sharhabeel bin 'Amr Al-Ghassani (the governor of Al-Balqa),which immediately led to the Battle of Mu'tah. But Mubarakpuri states that the event was one of the reasons behind the Battle of Tabouk as well.

Mubarakpuri further demonstrates that Heraclius, the emperor of the Byzantine Empire, was preparing a force to demolish the growing Muslim power in the region. Many rumors of the danger threatening the Muslims were carried to Mecca by Nabateans who traded from Syria to Madinah. They carried rumors of Heraclius' preparations and the existence of an enormous army which was said to number anywhere from 40,000 to several 100,000 besides the Lakhm, Judham and other Arab tribes allied with the Byzantines. After arriving at Tabouk and camping there, the Muslims army was prepared to face the Byzantines, still the Byzantines were not at Tabouk. They stayed there for a number of days and scouted the area but they never came.

Added to that, Jizyah is taken, according to ISIS, from non-Muslim citizens who live under the Muslim's rule; but the verse says "Fight", and a government of dominant majority doesn't fight minorities over taxes, it simply kill them. The verse, in this twisted understanding, comes to mean "Kill" or even "Murder" those who do not pay you Jizyah.

Jizyah, in its historical meaning, does not fit modern society, not only because it was imposed in a different political, social and economic situation in the history of Middle East. But rather because it affects the social structure of modern states. Let's take a modern Middle Eastern state which, hypothetically, enforces Jizyah on the Christians who constitute 20% of its population instead of the normal taxation system. Economically, 20% of the population would be paying far less taxes than the rest 80%; add to that, 20% of the population would not be serving in the army, which in addition to its impacts on defensive abilities, would be a disruption to the social order affecting relations between citizens of various religions.

ISIS Argument for Imposing Jizyah (Books of Islamic Heritage) :

Sulaiman bin Buraidah[22] reported on the authority of his father: When the Apostle of God appointed a Commander over an Army

---

[22] Sulaiman Ibn Buraidah (637?-727?) was a companion of Prophet Muhammad and a narrator of Hadith.

or a detachment, he instructed him to fear God himself and consider the welfare of the Muslims who were with him. He then said: *"When you meet the polytheists who are your enemy, summon them to one of three things. Summon them to Islam and if they agree, accept it from them and refrain from them.. If they refuse, demand Jizyah from them; if they agree accept it from them and refrain from them. But if they refuse, seek God's help and fight them.."* (Al-Sajistāni, 1999: 295).

This saying may be truly said by Prophet Muhammad if it was referring to an aggressor force. However, the relation between Muslims and other sects is organized by the following verse, and other likes: **(O you who have attained to faith! It is [but] for your own selves that you are responsible: those who go astray can do you no harm if you [yourselves] are on the right path. Unto God you all must return: and then He will make you [truly] understand all that you were doing [in life].)** Al-Maaedah 105.

Part 6: Apostasy

Apostasy was the major justification for terminating internal opposition throughout the history of Islamic empires. That is why we have heard of whole tribes and groups being eradicated for apostasy. Muslim philosophers, mathematicians and scientists were killed or exiled for apostasy and thus, the Muslim world stood still in all scientific and aesthetic fields.

Anyway, in the present time there are individuals who have been executed for apostasy in some Islamic countries such as: Saudi Arabia, Somalia and Iran. ISIS has been applying this twisted understanding on anyone opposes it, or even those who remained neutral and supported either side. But no, for ISIS you have to support their so-called caliph so as not to be punished for apostasy.

ISIS' Argument for the Punishment of Apostasy (from Quran):

([The hypocrites] swear by God that they have said nothing [wrong]; yet most certainly have they uttered a saying which amounts to a denial of the truth, and have [thus] denied the truth after [having professed] their self-surrender to God.. Hence, if they repent, it will be for their own good. but if they turn away, God will cause them to suffer grievous suffering in this world and in the life to come, and they will find no helper on earth, and none to give [them] succor.) Al-Tawba 74.

As a matter of fact, the verse above is talking about a group lived in Madinah with Muslims and told Prophet Muhammad that they are believers, whereas, really, they were not. That group tried to manipulate Muslims and persuade them back to unbelieving. Further, there is no mention of an earthly punishment that is carried by Muslims for unbelieving. Besides, if a person is to be punished for unbelieving in this life by ISIS or its jurists, would not it be unfair for God to punish that person again in the afterlife?

ISIS Argument for the Punishment of Apostasy (Books of Islamic Heritage):

There are many attributed-to-Prophet-Muhammad sayings in the books of Islamic heritage that promoting the punishment of apostasy. However, they are historically untrue, since there is no evidence that Prophet Muhammad killed anyone for apostasy. The Islamic empires, under their rule the books of Islamic heritage were written, made the greater use of such sayings in eliminating oppositions.

God's Messenger said: *"The blood of a Muslim who confesses that none has the right to be worshipped but God and that I am His Apostle, cannot be shed except in three cases: In Qisas [punishment] for murder, a married person who commits illegal sexual intercourse, and the one who reverts from Islam (apostate) and leaves the Muslims."* (Sahih Al-Bukhāri,1998: 1311).

Such sayings contradict other sayings, not to mention Quran, that are included in the same Islamic heritage books:

It has been narrated on the authority of Anas bin Malik that Quraish sent a group of their prestigious personalities to make peace, It is termed as Al-Hudaibiya Agreement (6 H),with the Prophet; among them was Suhail Ibn Amr. So, the Prophet said to Ali Ibn Abi Talib:

Write " In the name of God, most Gracious and most Merciful". Suhail said: As for" In the name of God" we do not know what is meant by" (In the name of God most Gracious and most Merciful). But write what we understand, i. e. "in thy name. O God". Then, the Prophet said: Write: " From Muhammad, the Messenger of God." They said: If we knew that you were the Messenger of God, we would follow you. Therefore, write your name and the name of your father. So the Prophet said: Write" From Muhammad Ibn Abdullah." They laid the condition on the Prophet that anyone who joined them from the Muslims, the Meccans would not return him, and anyone who joined you (the Muslims) from them, you would send him back to them. The Companions said: Messenger of God, should we write this? He said: Yes. One who goes away from us to join them-may God keep him away! and one who comes to join us from them (and is sent back) God will provide him relief and a way of escape. "(Sahih Muslim,2006: 859).

And thus, according to the same books Which ISIS theoreticians rely on to confirm the existence and legitimacy of apostasy punishment, there is a saying by Prophet Muhammad that includes: *"One who goes away from us to join them-may God keep him away."*

Chapter 3: Dismantling ISIS

Part 1: The Origin of ISIS

Is ISIS a Modern Organization?

The answer to this question would be: Yes and No. Yes, it is a modern organization in its tactics and strategies. It has filled the gabs and corrected the mistakes that were behind other organizations' destruction. ISIS is also modern in its military hierarchy, organization and techniques. It is modern in its peculiar method of using people's minds and infiltrating through the cracks between the peoples and their governments; using bad living situations, oppression of freedoms, and religious and sectarian tension. It is a modern organization in its consideration of the danger of competition, so before launching the war against the "apostate governments", it eliminated or engulfed other armed groups and organizations. ISIS' devious modernity became obvious when it declared the

Caliphate, even though it was on some scattered pieces of land; but ISIS had the knowledge that many ignorant extremists were waiting for this declaration. It gave them the hope they were longing for, and, with a successful propaganda, presented a bright image of life under the caliphate making it the destination to which all extremists marsh.

And No, ISIS is not a modern organization. It is an old view of Islam which has been founded and theorized by the Omayyad and Abbasside empires. When the Omayyad empire wanted to expand by taking more lands under its rule, it needed a holy cause for persuading people to support its plans. The new religion was the perfect cover, so it assigned the pro-state Islamic jurists to put the twisted sayings and issue their Fatwas (advisory opinions) for the public on the lawfulness of murdering, enslaving and invading non-Muslims. Internally, there were Fatwas for Obeying the ruler and the punishment of apostasy. Abbasside empire continued on the same track with differences that suited its needs. Whole tribes were eradicated for opposing the ruler under the apostasy punishment Fatwas; scientists, reformers, and jurists were executed for the same reason. Women were raped under the Fatwas of slavery; and captives were murdered or enslaved. The caliph became the shadow of God on earth and the sole ruler of people. Costumes and tradition took over again and became above the religion or an integral part of it.

Thus, ISIS was founded with the first saying that falsely attributed to Prophet Muhammad. It began its actions with the first extracted-from-context verse of Quran. And had it not been for Prophet Muhammad to command his followers to write the verses of Quran as soon as he recited them, they would also be twisted. Samih Asskar, a researcher in Islamic affairs, provides an interesting statistic in his article "Ibn Taymiyyah[23] and the Jurisprudence of Crime."

---

[23] Ibn Taymiyyah (1263-1328) was a Sunni Islamic scholar, Islamic philosopher,

Ibn Taymiyyah's Book "The Complete Fatwas" contained the following phrases:

"he either repents, or he should be killed" 75 times.

"he is an unbeliever" 111 times.

"he should be killed" 13 times.

"killing him is an obligation" 9 times.

"if he persisted, then he should be killed" once.

"he should be killed, as jurists agreed" once.

"it is allowed to kill him" twice.

"he is an apostate" 5 times.

"they either repent, or they should be killed." 3 times.

"he is an unbeliever, and his blood is shed in vain." Twice.

---

jurist, theologian and logician.

"he is a heretic." 4 times.

And as it is known for many people, Ibn Taymiyyah is one of the most quoted Islamic jurists by criminal organizations.

Part 2: How to Eradicate ISIS?

Undoubtedly, what has been taken by force will not be retrieved without force! ISIS as other tyrant occupation forces, is a foreign entity that invaded lands by the use of its force and the weakness of these land's defending forces and their abandonment to their people. And there is no chance to retrieve the occupied lands from ISIS peacefully.

Though, downsizing ISIS does not necessarily mean eradicating the intellect that produced it in the first place; we have seen organizations such as: Al-Qaida, Boko Haram, Abo Sayyaf and Al-Hijra wa Al-Jihad resurrecting again after their leaders had been killed and their militants scattered. Why these groups reborn again and again after being destroyed militarily? Because such groups are related to one way of thinking whether these groups are in India or in Nigeria; they depend on the same pretexts of the jurisprudence of crime and violence.

Hence, thinkers, reformers and researchers have to unify their ends to isolate and remove this understanding of Islam. The twisted understanding that is being fed to children in schools and being circulated through mosques. Many Islamic clerks are spreading the discourse of violence and the spirit of hatred; then they object on the actions of ISIS! They are producing ISIS generation by another, throughout their discourse and curricula. ISIS also knows how important spreading its way of thinking is; and here it has started copying and imposing its own curricula all over the schools under its power.

ISIS is not a mere criminal organization that spreads death wherever it went, it is rather a crisis of a nation. A nation following a twisted ugly jurisprudence which has been written as a guidance for the ruler of a strong political state. To destroy ISIS, before it destroys what is left of Islam, Muslims badly need to take some brave steps such as:

1- Following Quran as it is, clear and simple; without relying on the violent interpretations and criminal desires of radical Islamists.

2- Locating the flaws in the books of Islamic heritage, and getting rid of whatever contradicts the Quran and human values.

3- Filtering out hatred and discourse of violence from school and university curricula.

4- Establishing a well-defined Islamic moral philosophy. Islamic world needs a moral revolution as well as well-cut values; and that will not be possible without a clear plan to raise up a generation that respect others' values and freedoms.

5- In the present time, Muslims have many great reformers among them. Supporting those reformers would be a big step towards eradicating criminal groups and showing the true tolerant face of Islam.

These steps may be the beginning to a reformation revolution that puts an end to the expansion of radical criminal organizations.

Organizations such as ISIS have murdered and displaced way more Muslims than any other "enemy" has ever done. Intellectual movements would also contribute to spreading a positive discourse and an objective way of thinking, showing people the downsides of religious, sectarian and racial conflicts.

The uneducated or half-educated public is what ISIS targets; and so reformation currents should do. The mission of eradicating radical Islamists is not limited to intellectuals and jurists, but rather extends to every member of the Muslim community. A Facebook post, a tweet on Twitter or a chat in a coffee shop would be a great contribution to alerting the people to the danger of criminal organizations and the way they use religion to cover up their rotten desires.

Conclusion:

The first two chapters of this book have been put in an order that explains the cause-effect relation between criminal organizations' actions and the pretexts being used to justify those actions. Following this approach, the first chapter was an introductory one, bringing to light some of the vagueness of the books of Islamic heritage; especially books of Hadith and the circumstances under which they were written; those books which contain many of the justifications criminal organization use. The first chapter also presented some of the historical facts that disqualify the books of Islamic heritage as a respectable source of religion or legislation. Criminal organizations use some off-context verses of Quran as well, presenting them as solid commands to killing, enslaving, torturing and raping people. However, a contextual reading of these verses would make it clear that criminal organizations have been manipulating people's minds for centuries. The case is different with the books of Islamic heritage, since these books were originally written in the propose of waging wars against other states and empires during Omayyad and Abbasside reigns centuries after Prophet Muhammad's death; and this is why many Muslim reformers and thinkers are calling for considering those books as books of heritage and not a source of legislation. Another point to consider, many of the Hadiths ISIS quotes outrightly contradict clear verses of Quran. There may be some Hadiths that are really said by Prophet Muhammad, however, they were mere exercise of judgments in particular cases by Prophet Muhammad as the leader of his community then.

The second chapter was devoted to some of the actions of criminal organizations, in this case ISIS, in the name of Islam, and the weak arguments they present defending their actions. ISIS has been doing many unthinkable things in the lands it invaded in Iraq and Syria. The chapter focused on the most despicable actions and the devious arguments for them. It also discussed the Quran verses that have been being intentionally misquoted by criminal organizations such as ISIS. The ill interpretations of some of Quran verses were a great aid to the ISIS ideology along the course of history.

The third chapter discussed how to dismantle ISIS. It did not explore how to dismantle the infamous organization militarily, however, it tackled the ideological side of ISIS, and the environment in which ISIS flourishes and thrives. The third chapter also presented some steps that are being shyly taken to dwarf the influence of this extremist ideology. And since the emergence of ISIS is no surprise, but rather a result of centuries of twisted presentation of Islam; so the most suitable approach to dismantle ISIS is an intellectual and ideological one, by clearing the misunderstanding of Quran verses and clearing out the worship of Islamic heritage books.

References:

Al-Bukhāri, Muhammad. (1998). Sahih Al-Bukhāri. Amman & Al-Riyādh: Bait Al-'afkār Al-Dwaliyya Publications.

Al-Ghazāli, Muhammad. (2000). Fiqh Al-Seera. Cairo: Dār Al-Shurooq Publications.

Al-Muttaqi, Aladdin. (1989). Kanzul'Ummāl (Part.1).Beirut: Al-Resala Publications

Al-Neesabouri, Muslim.(2006). Sahih Muslim (Vol.2). Al- Riyādh: Dār Teeba Publications

Al-Sajistāni, Sulaimān. (1999). Sunan Abi Dā'oud. Amman & Al-Riyādh: Bait Al-'afkār Al-Duwaliyya Publications

Al-Tahhān, Mahmoud. (1995). Tayseer Mustalah Al-Hadith. Al-Mada for Studies.

Al-Thahabi, Shamsuddin. (1374). Tathkirat-lhuffādh (Vol.1). Hyderabad: Dā'irat Al-Ma'ārif Al-Othmāniyya.

Al-Tirmithi, Muhammad. (1999). J̄ami' Al-Tirmithi. Amman & Al-Riyādh: Bait Al-'afkār Al-Duwaliyya Publications

'Askar, Samih. (2014). Ibn Taymiya and the Jurisprudence of Crime. Available at: http://www.ahl-alquran.com/arabic/show_article.php?main_id=11757

'Awwād, Georges. (1982). Aqdam Al-Makhtootat Al-Arabiyya fi Maktabāt Al-'ālam. Baghdad: Al-Rasheed Publications

Hasan, Ammar Ali. (2012). "Introduction", in Abdulraziq, Ali Al-Islam wa 'Usool Al-Hukm. Alexandria: Alexandria Library Publications. Pp.19-77

Jum'ah, Ibraheem.(1981). Qissat Al-Kitāba Al-Arabiyya. Cairo: Dār Al-Ma'ārif Publications

Mar'i, Abdullah. (2003). Ahkām Al-Mujāhid bil-Nafs fil- fiqh Al-Islāmi. Medina: Al-'Uloom wal Hikam Library.

No Author. (2014). "The Revival of Slavery before the Hour", in Dabiq (Issue. 4). Al-Hayat Media Establishment. Available at: http://dc310.gulfup.com/ohxq99.pdf?gu=YSo ImEmJZjGWOW40GZdDoA&e=142434200 7&n=66696c656e616d652a3d5554462d3827 2744616269715f30345f656e2e706466

Qaddouri, Ghanim. (2003). Muhazarāt fi 'Uloom Al-Quran. Amman: Dār Ammār Publications

Rahman Al-Mubarakpuri, Saifur. (2007). Al-Raheek Al-Makhtoom. Publications of the Ministry of Islamic Affairs in Qatar.

Shahrour, Muhammad. (1994). A Comment on the Books, Articles, and Responses to "The Book and Quran: Contemporary Reading". Available at: http://www.shahrour.org/?page_id=550